The Markdown Guide

Matt Cone

The Markdown Guide

Matt Cone

ISBN 9798656504492

To Simon Naseem

Contents

CONTENTS

Introduction

I'm a technical writer, and I've used a lot of writing tools over the course of my professional career. One of the most interesting tools I've encountered is a markup language called Markdown.

My litmus test for a successful writing tool is whether using it can become second nature. Does writing with it feel natural? Or do I feel like I'm constantly fighting against it? I stop using tools that hinder me. Time is valuable, and I don't have the luxury of indulging things that squander that precious resource.

Markdown passes the test with flying colors. Writing using Markdown just *feels right*. Since its introduction in 2004, millions of people have started using it to write everything from notes to documents. It's one of the most successful markup languages of all time.

Markdown has succeeded where other markup languages have failed because it strikes the right balance between power and simplicity. It's easy to learn and simple to use. Its tremendous success means it's ubiquitous enough to replace WYSIWYG editors on websites like Reddit and GitHub. But Markdown is also powerful enough to create documents, books, and technical documentation. Markdown is literally everywhere.

I've been using Markdown for years now and I recommend it to everyone I know. There are lots of reasons why you should learn to write using Markdown, but one of the best reasons is that it's better than the alternatives. Learning Markdown means you can stop using all the subpar writing tools you've tolerated for years. It can also further your career. Believe it or not, knowing how to write using Markdown is a requirement for many jobs.

That brings us to this book. I couldn't find a comprehensive Markdown reference guide, so I decided to create one.

The Markdown Guide has humble beginnings. It started as a single webpage[1] in 2017. After receiving positive feedback from friends and coworkers, I decided to expand the site. To my astonishment, *The Markdown Guide* was receiving hundreds of unique visitors a day by early 2018. At that point, it occurred to me that people might also appreciate *The Markdown Guide* in book format.

I hope you enjoy reading this book as much as I've enjoyed writing it. Above all, I hope it helps you write using Markdown, and I hope using Markdown makes you a better writer.

How to Read This Book

This book is designed to be a comprehensive reference guide to the Markdown markup language. If you're new to Markdown, start at the beginning and read to the end. If you're an expert user, keep this book handy — you never know when you'll need to refer back to the cheat sheet at the end of the book.

Beginner Resources

The first two chapters of this book are designed exclusively for readers who are new to Markdown. Getting Started provides a quick introduction to Markdown. It shows you how to get going quickly with the Dillinger online Markdown editor, and it sheds light on some of the stuff going on behind the scenes.

Doing Things With Markdown talks about what you can create using Markdown. It also presents some of the applications you can use to write Markdown.

---

[1]https://www.markdownguide.org/

Syntax Examples

To help you learn how to write using Markdown, I've provided three sections for every syntax element in the chapters on basic and extended syntax:

- **Markdown**: This is what you'll type in your Markdown application.
- **HTML**: This is the HTML code that'll be generated by the Markdown processor.
- **Rendered Output**: This is what the reader will see.

To learn more about the Markdown to HTML conversion, see the section on how Markdown works in Chapter 1.

Asides

Extra bits of information are displayed with an "i" icon next to them, like this:

 Here's some extra information you might find helpful.

Tips are displayed with a key icon next to them, like this:

 Here's a cool tip you might find useful.

Quirks

Some of the Markdown and HTML code samples in this book "wrap" to the next line. In the situations where that happens, you'll see a \ at the end of the first line of the code block. That \ isn't actually part of the code. It's displayed there to indicate that the next line of the code block is actually part of the same line.

Acknowledgements

I'm eternally grateful to Reem and our children, Finn and Simon. This book wouldn't exist without their love and support.

I greatly appreciate the help of AK Molteni, Gaylin Walli, Juan Torrez, Diana Lynch, and my parents, Steve Cone and Kathie Lathan, who were sounding boards for the website and book. Thanks to Josh Ellingson for creating the amazing, jaw-dropping artwork on the cover. Last, but certainly not least, I'd like to thank *you* and everyone else who has read and contributed to *The Markdown Guide*. You've not only made this book possible, you've made it better!

1. Getting Started

Markdown is a lightweight markup language that you can use to add formatting elements to plaintext text documents. Created by John Gruber in 2004, Markdown is now one of the world's most popular markup languages.

Using Markdown is different than using a WYSIWYG ("What You See Is What You Get") editor. In an application like Microsoft Word, you click buttons to format words and phrases, and the changes are visible immediately. Markdown isn't like that. When you create a Markdown-formatted file, you add Markdown syntax to the text to indicate which words and phrases should look different.

For example, to denote a heading, you add a number sign before it (e.g., # Heading One). Or to make a phrase bold, you add two asterisks before and after it (e.g., **this text is bold**). It may take a while to get used to seeing Markdown syntax in your text, especially if you're accustomed to WYSIWYG applications. The screenshot below shows a Markdown file displayed in the Atom text editor[1].

This is a Markdown file in the Atom text editor.

You can add Markdown formatting elements to a plaintext file using a text editor application. Or you can use one of the many Markdown applications for macOS, Windows, Linux, iOS, and Android

---

[1]https://atom.io

operating systems. There are also several web-based applications specifically designed for writing in Markdown.

Depending on the application you use, you may not be able to preview the formatted document in real time. But that's okay. According to Gruber, Markdown syntax is designed to be readable and unobtrusive, so the text in Markdown files can be read even if it isn't rendered.

> The overriding design goal for Markdown's formatting syntax is to make it as readable as possible. The idea is that a Markdown-formatted document should be publishable as-is, as plain text, without looking like it's been marked up with tags or formatting instructions.

Why Use Markdown?

You might be wondering why people use Markdown instead of a WYSIWYG editor. Why write with Markdown when you can press buttons in an interface to format your text? As it turns out, there are a couple different reasons why people use Markdown instead of WYSIWYG editors.

- Markdown can be used for everything. People use it to create websites, documents, notes, books, presentations, email messages, and technical documentation.
- Markdown is portable. Files containing Markdown-formatted text can be opened using virtually any application. If you decide you don't like the Markdown application you're currently using, you can import your Markdown files into another Markdown application. That's in stark contrast to word processing applications like Microsoft Word that lock your content into a proprietary file format.

- Markdown is platform independent. You can create Markdown-formatted text on any device running any operating system.
- Markdown is future proof. Even if the application you're using stops working at some point in the future, you'll still be able to read your Markdown-formatted text using a text editing application. This is an important consideration when it comes to books, university theses, and other milestone documents that need to be preserved indefinitely.
- Markdown is everywhere. Websites like Reddit and GitHub support Markdown, and lots of desktop and web-based applications support it.

Kicking the Tires

The best way to get started with Markdown is to use it. That's easier than ever before thanks to a variety of free tools.

You don't even need to download anything. There are several online Markdown editors that you can use to try writing in Markdown. Dillinger[2] is one of the best online Markdown editors. Just open the site and start typing in the left pane. A preview of the rendered document appears in the right pane.

---

[2] https://dillinger.io/

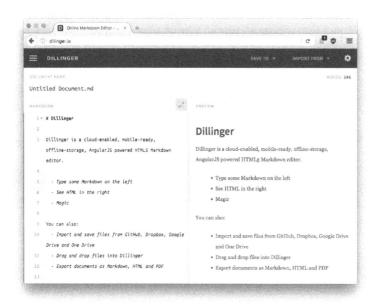

The Dillinger Markdown editor is a free and easy way to get started with Markdown.

You'll probably want to keep the Dillinger website open as you read through this guide. That way you can try the syntax as you learn about it. After you've become familiar with Markdown, you may want to use a Markdown application that can be installed on your desktop computer or mobile device.

How Markdown Works

Dillinger makes writing in Markdown easy because it hides the stuff happening behind the scenes, but it's worth exploring how the process works in general.

When you write in Markdown, the text is stored in a plaintext file that has an .md or .markdown extension. But then what? How is your Markdown-formatted file converted into HTML or a print-ready document?

The short answer is that you need a *Markdown application* capable of processing the Markdown file. There are lots of applications available — everything from simple scripts to desktop applications that look like Microsoft Word. Despite their visual differences, all of the applications do the same thing. Like Dillinger, they all convert Markdown-formatted text to HTML so it can be displayed in web browsers.

Markdown applications use something called a *Markdown processor* (also commonly referred to as a "parser" or an "implementation") to take the Markdown-formatted text and output it to HTML format. At that point, your document can be viewed in a web browser or combined with a style sheet and printed. You can see a visual representation of this process below.

 The Markdown application and processor are two separate components. For the sake of brevity, I've combined them into one element ("Markdown App") in the figure below.

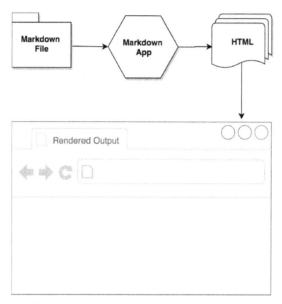

This is a visual overview of the Markdown process.

To summarize, this is a four-part process:

1. Create a Markdown file using a text editor or a dedicated Markdown application. The file should have an .md or .mark-down extension.
2. Open the Markdown file in a Markdown application.
3. Use the Markdown application to convert the Markdown file to an HTML document.
4. View the HTML file in a web browser or use the Markdown application to convert it to another file format, like PDF.

From your perspective, the process will vary somewhat depending on the application you use. For example, Dillinger essentially combines steps 1-3 into a single, seamless interface — all you have to do is type in the left pane and the rendered output magically appears in the right pane. But if you use other tools, like a text editor with a static website generator, you'll find that the process is much more visible.

Flavors of Markdown

One of the most confusing aspects of using Markdown is that practically every Markdown application implements a slightly different version of Markdown. These variants of Markdown are commonly referred to as *flavors*. It's your job to master whatever flavor of Markdown your application has implemented.

To wrap your head around the concept of Markdown flavors, it might help to think of them as language dialects. People in New York City speak English just like the people in London, but there are substantial differences between the dialects used in both cities. The same is true for people using different Markdown applications. Using Dillinger[3] to write with Markdown is a vastly different experience than using Ulysses[4].

Practically speaking, this means you never know exactly what a company means when they say they support "Markdown." Are they talking about only the basic syntax elements, or all of the basic and extended syntax elements combined, or some arbitrary combination of syntax elements? You won't know until you read the documentation or start using the application.

If you're just starting out, the best advice I can give you is to pick a Markdown application with good Markdown support. That'll go a long way towards maintaining the portability of your Markdown files. You might want to store and use your Markdown files in other applications, and to do that you need to start with an application that provides good support. You can use the Markdown tool directory[5] to find an application that fits the bill.

---

[3]https://www.markdownguide.org/tools/dillinger/
[4]https://www.markdownguide.org/tools/ulysses/
[5]https://www.markdownguide.org/tools/

Additional Resources

There are lots of other resources you can use to learn Markdown. Here are a few of my favorites:

- John Gruber's Markdown documentation[6]. The original guide written by the creator of Markdown.
- Markdown Tutorial[7]. An open source website that allows you to try Markdown in your web browser.
- Awesome Markdown[8]. A list of Markdown tools and learning resources.
- Typesetting Markdown[9]. A multi-part series that describes an ecosystem for typesetting Markdown documents using pandoc[10] and ConTeXt[11].

---

[6]https://daringfireball.net/projects/markdown/
[7]https://www.markdowntutorial.com/
[8]https://github.com/mundimark/awesome-markdown
[9]https://dave.autonoma.ca/blog/2019/05/22/typesetting-markdown-part-1
[10]https://pandoc.org/
[11]https://www.contextgarden.net/

2. Doing Things With Markdown

Now that you know what Markdown is, you're probably wondering what you can do with it. The answer is: just about anything. Markdown is a fast and easy way to take notes, create content for a website, and produce print-ready documents.

It doesn't take long to learn the Markdown syntax, and once you know how to use it, you can write using Markdown just about everywhere. Most people use Markdown to create content for the web, but Markdown is good for formatting everything from email messages to grocery lists.

Here are some examples of what you can do with Markdown.

Websites

Markdown was designed for the web, so it should come as no surprise that there are plenty of applications specifically designed for creating website content.

If you're looking for the simplest possible way to create a website with Markdown files, check out blot.im[1]. After you sign up for Blot, it creates a Dropbox folder on your computer. Just drag and drop your Markdown files into the folder and — poof! — they're on your website. It couldn't be easier.

If you're familiar with HTML, CSS, and version control, check out Jekyll[2], a popular static site generator that takes Markdown files and

---

[1]https://blot.im
[2]https://jekyllrb.com/

builds an HTML website. One advantage to this approach is that GitHub Pages[3] provides free hosting for Jekyll-generated websites. If Jekyll isn't your cup of tea, just pick one of the many other static site generators available[4].

 I used Jekyll to create the Markdown Guide website[5]. You can view the source code on GitHub[6].

If you'd like to use a content management system (CMS) to power your website, take a look at Ghost[7]. It's a free and open-source blogging platform with a nice Markdown editor. If you're a Word-Press user, you'll be happy to know there's Markdown support for websites hosted on WordPress.com. Self-hosted WordPress sites can use the Jetpack plugin[8].

Documents

Markdown doesn't have all the bells and whistles of word processors like Microsoft Word, but it's good enough for creating basic documents like assignments and letters. You can use a Markdown document authoring application to create and export Markdown-formatted documents to PDF or HTML file format. The PDF part is key, because once you have a PDF document, you can do anything with it — print it, email it, or upload it to a website.

Here are some Markdown document authoring applications I recommend:

---

[3]https://pages.github.com/
[4]https://www.staticgen.com/
[5]https://www.markdownguide.org
[6]https://github.com/mattcone/markdown-guide
[7]https://ghost.org/
[8]https://jetpack.com/support/markdown/

- **Mac:** MacDown[9], iA Writer[10], or Marked 2[11]
- **iOS / Android:** iA Writer[12]
- **Windows:** ghostwriter[13] or Markdown Monster[14]
- **Linux:** ReText[15] or ghostwriter[16]
- **Web:** Dillinger[17] or StackEdit[18]

 iA Writer provides templates[19] for previewing, printing, and exporting Markdown-formatted documents. For example, the "Academic – MLA Style" template indents paragraphs and adds double sentence spacing.

Notes

In nearly every way, Markdown is the ideal syntax for taking notes. Sadly, Evernote[20] and OneNote[21], two of the most popular note applications, don't currently support Markdown. The good news is that several other note applications *do* support Markdown:

- Simplenote[22] is a free, barebones note-taking application available for every platform.

[9]https://macdown.uranusjr.com/
[10]https://ia.net/writer/
[11]https://marked2app.com/
[12]https://ia.net/writer/
[13]https://wereturtle.github.io/ghostwriter/
[14]https://markdownmonster.west-wind.com/
[15]https://github.com/retext-project/retext
[16]https://wereturtle.github.io/ghostwriter/
[17]https://dillinger.io
[18]https://stackedit.io/
[19]https://ia.net/writer/templates
[20]https://evernote.com/
[21]https://www.onenote.com/
[22]https://simplenote.com/

- Notable[23] is a note-taking application that runs on a variety of platforms.
- Bear[24] is an Evernote-like application available for Mac and iOS devices. It doesn't exclusively use Markdown syntax by default, but you can enable Markdown compatibility mode.
- Joplin[25] is a note taking application that respects your privacy. It's available for every platform.
- Boostnote[26] bills itself as an "open source note-taking app designed for programmers."

If you can't part with Evernote, check out Marxico[27], a subscription-based Markdown editor for Evernote, or use Markdown Here[28] with the Evernote website.

Books

Looking to self-publish a novel? Try Leanpub[29], a service that takes your Markdown-formatted files and turns them into an electronic book. Leanpub outputs your book in PDF, EPUB, and MOBI file format. If you'd like to create paperback copies of your book, you can upload the PDF file to another service such as Kindle Direct Publishing[30].

Presentations

Believe it or not, you can generate presentations from Markdown-formatted files. Creating presentations in Markdown takes a little

---

[23]https://notable.md
[24]https://bear.app/
[25]https://joplinapp.org/
[26]https://boostnote.io/
[27]https://marxi.co/
[28]https://markdown-here.com/features.html#not-just-email
[29]https://leanpub.com/
[30]https://kdp.amazon.com

getting used to, but once you get the hang of it, it's a lot faster and easier than using an application like PowerPoint or Keynote. Remark[31] (GitHub project[32]) is a popular browser-based Markdown slideshow tool, as are Cleaver[33] (GitHub project[34]) and Marp[35] (GitHub project[36]). If you use a Mac and would prefer to use an application, check out Deckset[37] or Hyperdeck[38].

Email

If you send a lot of email and you're tired of the formatting controls available on most email provider websites, you'll be happy to learn there's an easy way to write email messages using Markdown. Markdown Here[39] is a free and open-source browser extension that converts Markdown-formatted text into HTML that's ready to send.

Collaboration

Collaboration and team messaging applications are a popular way of communicating with coworkers and friends at work and home. These applications don't utilize all of Markdown's features, but the features they do provide are fairly useful. For example, the ability to bold and italicize text without using the WYSIWYG interface is pretty handy. Slack[40], Discord[41], Wiki.js[42], and Mattermost[43] are all

---

[31]https://remarkjs.com
[32]https://github.com/gnab/remark
[33]https://jdan.github.io/cleaver/
[34]https://github.com/jdan/cleaver
[35]https://marp.app/
[36]https://github.com/marp-team/marp
[37]https://www.decksetapp.com/
[38]https://hyperdeck.io/
[39]https://markdown-here.com
[40]https://slack.com
[41]https://discord.com
[42]https://js.wiki
[43]https://mattermost.com

good collaboration applications.

Documentation

Markdown is a natural fit for technical documentation. Companies like GitHub are increasingly switching to Markdown for their documentation — check out their blog post[44] about how they migrated their Markdown-formatted documentation to Jekyll[45]. If you write documentation for a product or service, take a look at these handy tools:

- Read the Docs[46] can generate a documentation website from your open source Markdown files. Just connect your GitHub repository to their service and push — Read the Docs does the rest. They also have a service for commercial entities.
- MkDocs[47] is a fast and simple static site generator that's geared towards building documentation. The source files are written in Markdown and organized with a single YAML configuration file. MkDocs has several built in themes, including a port of the Read the Docs documentation theme. One of the newest themes is MkDocs Material, which incorporates elements of Google's Material Design.
- Docusaurus[48] is a static site generator designed exclusively for creating documentation websites. It supports translations, search, and versioning.
- VuePress[49] is a static site generator powered by Vue and optimized for writing technical documentation.
- Jekyll[50] was mentioned earlier in the section on websites, but it's also a good option for generating a documentation

---

[44]https://github.com/blog/1939-how-github-uses-github-to-document-github
[45]https://jekyllrb.com/
[46]https://readthedocs.org
[47]https://www.mkdocs.org/
[48]https://docusaurus.io/
[49]https://vuepress.vuejs.org/
[50]https://jekyllrb.com/

website from Markdown files. If you go this route, be sure to check out the Jekyll documentation theme[51].

---

[51]https://idratherbewriting.com/documentation-theme-jekyll/

3. Basic Syntax

Nearly all Markdown applications support the basic syntax outlined in John Gruber's original design document. There are minor variations and discrepancies between Markdown processors — those are noted inline wherever possible.

Headings

To create a heading, add number signs (#) in front of a word or phrase. The number of number signs you use should correspond to the heading level. For example, to create a heading level three (<h3>), use three number signs (e.g., ### My Header).

Markdown	HTML
# Heading level 1	<h1>Heading level 1</h1>
## Heading level 2	<h2>Heading level 2</h2>
### Heading level 3	<h3>Heading level 3</h3>
#### Heading level 4	<h4>Heading level 4</h4>
##### Heading level 5	<h5>Heading level 5</h5>
###### Heading level 6	<h6>Heading level 6</h6>

Alternate Syntax

Alternatively, on the line below the text, add any number of == characters for heading level 1 or -- characters for heading level 2.

Markdown	HTML
```Heading level 1```	```<h1>Heading level 1</h1>```
```===============```	
```Heading level 2```	```<h2>Heading level 2</h2>```
```---------------```	

Heading Best Practices

Markdown applications don't agree on how to handle a missing space between the number signs (#) and the heading name. For compatibility, always put a space between the number signs and the heading name.

Do this	Don't do this
```# Here's a Heading```	```#Here's a Heading```

You should also put blank lines before and after a heading for compatibility.

Do this	Don't do this
```Try to put a blank line before...```	```Without blank lines, this might not look right.```
	```# Heading```
```# Heading```	```Don't do this!```
```...and after a heading.```	

Paragraphs

To create paragraphs, use a blank line to separate one or more lines of text.

Markdown

```
I really like using Markdown.

I think I'll use it from now on.
```

HTML

```
<p>I really like using Markdown.</p>

<p>I think I'll use it from now on.</p>
```

The rendered output looks like this:

I really like using Markdown.

I think I'll use it from now on.

Paragraph Best Practices

Unless the paragraph is in a list, don't indent paragraphs with spaces or tabs.

Do this	Don't do this
`Don't put tabs or spaces in front of your paragraphs.`	`This can result in unexpected formatting problems.`
`Keep lines left-aligned like this.`	`Don't add tabs or spaces in front of paragraphs.`

Line Breaks

To create a line break (`<br>`), end a line with two or more spaces, and then type return.

Markdown
```
This is the first line.
And this is the second line.
```

HTML
```
<p>This is the first line.<br />
And this is the second line.</p>
```

The rendered output looks like this:

This is the first line.
And this is the second line.

Line Break Best Practices

You can use two or more spaces (commonly referred to as "trailing whitespace") for line breaks in nearly every Markdown application, but it's controversial. It's hard to see trailing whitespace in an editor, and many people accidentally or intentionally put two spaces after every sentence. For this reason, you may want to use something other than trailing whitespace for line breaks. If your Markdown application supports HTML, you can use the `<br>` HTML tag.

For compatibility, use trailing white space or the `<br>` HTML tag at the end of the line.

There are two other options I don't recommend using. Common-Mark and a few other lightweight markup languages let you type a backslash (\) at the end of the line, but not all Markdown applications support this, so it isn't a great option from a compatibility perspective. And at least a couple lightweight markup languages don't require anything at the end of the line — just type return and they'll create a line break.

Do this	Don't do this
| ```
First line with two
spaces after.
And the next line.
``` | ```
First line with a
backslash after.\
And the next line.
``` |
| ```
With the HTML tag
after.<br>
And the next line.
``` | ```
With nothing after.

And the next line.
``` |

Emphasis

You can add emphasis by making text bold or italic.

Bold

To bold text, add two asterisks or underscores before and after a word or phrase. To bold the middle of a word for emphasis, add two asterisks without spaces around the letters.

Markdown
```
I love **bold text**.

I love __bold text__.

Love**is**bold
```

The HTML output of the first two examples is the same.

HTML
```
I love <strong>bold text</strong>.

Love<strong>is</strong>bold
```

The rendered output looks like this:

I love **bold text**.

Love**is**bold

Bold Best Practices

Markdown applications don't agree on how to handle underscores in the middle of a word. For compatibility, use asterisks to bold the middle of a word for emphasis.

Do this	Don't do this
Love**is**bold	Love__is__bold

Italic

To italicize text, add one asterisk or underscore before and after a word or phrase. To italicize the middle of a word for emphasis, add one asterisk without spaces around the letters.

Markdown

```
The *cat's meow*.

The _cat's meow_.

A*cat*meow
```

The HTML output of the first two examples is the same.

HTML

```
The <em>cat's meow</em>.

A<em>cat</em>meow
```

The rendered output looks like this:

The *cat's meow*.

A*cat*meow

Italic Best Practices

Markdown applications don't agree on how to handle underscores in the middle of a word. For compatibility, use asterisks to italicize the middle of a word for emphasis.

Do this	Don't do this
A*cat*meow	A_cat_meow

Bold and Italic

To emphasize text with bold and italics at the same time, add three asterisks or underscores before and after a word or phrase. To bold and italicize the middle of a word for emphasis, add three asterisks without spaces around the letters.

Markdown

```
***Important*** text.

___Important___ text.

__*Important*__ text.

**_Important_** text.

Really***very***important text.
```

The HTML output of the first four examples is the same.

HTML

```
<strong><em>Important</em></strong> text.

Really<strong><em>very</em></strong>important text.
```

The rendered output looks like this:

Important text.

Really*very*important text.

Bold and Italic Best Practices

Markdown applications don't agree on how to handle underscores in the middle of a word. For compatibility, use asterisks to bold and italicize the middle of a word for emphasis.

Do this	Don't do this
`Really***very***important text.`	`Really___very___-important text.`

Blockquotes

To create a blockquote, add a › in front of a paragraph.

Markdown
```
> Dorothy followed her through many rooms.
```

HTML
```
<blockquote>
  <p>Dorothy followed her through many rooms.</p>
</blockquote>
```

The rendered output looks like this:

> Dorothy followed her through many rooms.

Blockquotes with Multiple Paragraphs

Blockquotes can contain multiple paragraphs. Add a › on the blank lines between the paragraphs.

Markdown

```
> This the first paragraph.
>
> And this is the second paragraph.
```

HTML

```
<blockquote>
  <p>This the first paragraph.</p>
  <p>And this is the second paragraph.</p>
</blockquote>
```

The rendered output looks like this:

> This the first paragraph.
>
> And this is the second paragraph.

Nested Blockquotes

Blockquotes can be nested. Add a >> in front of the paragraph you want to nest.

Markdown

```
> This the first paragraph.
>
>> And this is the nested paragraph.
```

HTML

```
<blockquote>
  <p>This the first paragraph.</p>
  <blockquote>
    <p>And this is the nested paragraph.</p>
  </blockquote>
</blockquote>
```

The rendered output looks like this:

> This the first paragraph.
>
> > And this is the nested paragraph.

Blockquotes with Other Elements

Blockquotes can contain other Markdown formatted elements. Not all elements can be used — you'll need to experiment to see which ones work.

Markdown

```
> ##### The quarterly results look great!
>
> - Revenue was off the chart.
> - Profits were higher than ever.
>
>   *Everything* is going **well**.
```

HTML

```
<blockquote>
  <h5>The quarterly results look great!</h5>
  <ul>
    <li>Revenue was off the chart.</li>
    <li>Profits were higher than ever.</li>
  </ul>
  <p><em>Everything</em> is going <strong>well</strong>.<\
/p>
</blockquote>
```

The rendered output looks like this:

The quarterly results look great!

- Revenue was off the chart.
- Profits were higher than ever.

Everything is going **well**.

Blockquotes Best Practices

For compatibility, put blank lines before and after blockquotes.

Do this	Don't do this
Try to put a blank line before...	Without blank lines, this might not look right. > This is a blockquote
> This is a blockquote	Don't do this!
...and after a blockquote.	

Lists

You can organize items into ordered and unordered lists.

Ordered Lists

To create an ordered list, add line items with numbers followed by periods. The numbers don't have to be in numerical order, but the list should start with the number one.

Markdown

```
1. First item
2. Second item
3. Third item
4. Fourth item
```

```
1. First item
1. Second item
1. Third item
1. Fourth item
```

```
1. First item
8. Second item
3. Third item
5. Fourth item
```

The HTML output of all three example lists is the same.

HTML

```
<ol>
  <li>First item</li>
  <li>Second item</li>
  <li>Third item</li>
  <li>Fourth item</li>
</ol>
```

The rendered output looks like this:

1. First item
2. Second item
3. Third item
4. Fourth item

Nesting List Items

To nest line items in an ordered list, indent the items four spaces or one tab.

Markdown

```
1. First item
2. Second item
3. Third item
    1. Indented item
    2. Indented item
4. Fourth item
```

HTML

```
<ol>
  <li>First item</li>
  <li>Second item</li>
  <li>Third item
    <ol>
      <li>Indented item</li>
      <li>Indented item</li>
    </ol>
  </li>
  <li>Fourth item</li>
</ol>
```

The rendered output looks like this:

1. First item
2. Second item
3. Third item
    1. Indented item
    2. Indented item
4. Fourth item

Ordered List Best Practices

CommonMark and a few other lightweight markup languages let you use a parenthesis ()) as a delimiter (e.g., `1) First item`), but not all Markdown applications support this, so it isn't a great option from a compatibility perspective. For compatibility, use periods only.

Do this	Don't do this
`1. First item`	`1) First item`
`2. Second item`	`2) Second item`

Unordered Lists

To create an unordered list, add dashes (-), asterisks (*), or plus signs (+) in front of line items.

Markdown
```
- First item
- Second item
- Third item
- Fourth item

* First item
* Second item
* Third item
* Fourth item

+ First item
+ Second item
+ Third item
+ Fourth item
```

The HTML output of all three example lists is the same.

HTML
```
<ul>
  <li>First item</li>
  <li>Second item</li>
  <li>Third item</li>
  <li>Fourth item </li>
</ul>
```

The rendered output looks like this:

- First item
- Second item
- Third item
- Fourth item

Nesting List Items

To nest line items in an unordered list, indent the items four spaces or one tab.

Markdown

```
- First item
- Second item
- Third item
    - Indented item
    - Indented item
- Fourth item
```

HTML

```
<ul>
  <li>First item</li>
  <li>Second item</li>
  <li>Third item
    <ul>
      <li>Indented item</li>
      <li>Indented item</li>
    </ul>
  </li>
  <li>Fourth item</li>
</ul>
```

The rendered output looks like this:

- First item
- Second item
- Third item
    - Indented item
    - Indented item
- Fourth item

Starting Unordered List Items With Numbers

If you need to start an unordered list item with a number followed by a period, you can use a backslash (\) to escape the period.

Markdown

```
- 1968\. A great year!
- I think 1969 was second best.
```

HTML

```
<ul>
  <li>1968. A great year!</li>
  <li>I think 1969 was second best.</li>
</ul>
```

The rendered output looks like this:

- 1968. A great year!
- I think 1969 was second best.

Unordered List Best Practices

Markdown applications don't agree on how to handle different delimiters in the same list. For compatibility, don't mix and match delimiters in the same list — pick one and stick with it.

Do this	Don't do this
- First item	+ First item
- Second item	* Second item
- Third item	- Third item
- Fourth item	+ Fourth item

Adding Elements in Lists

To add another element in a list while preserving the continuity of
the list, indent the element four spaces or one tab, as shown in the
following examples.

 If things don't appear the way you expect, double
check that you've indented the elements in the list
four spaces or one tab.

Paragraphs

Markdown

```
* This is the first list item.
* Here's the second list item.

    I need to add another paragraph below the second list\
  item.

* And here's the third list item.
```

HTML

```
<ul>
  <li><p>This is the first list item.</p></li>
  <li><p>Here's the second list item.</p>
    <p>I need to add another paragraph below the second l\
ist item.</p>
  </li>
  <li><p>And here's the third list item.</p></li>
</ul>
```

The rendered output looks like this:

- This is the first list item.
- Here's the second list item.

  I need to add another paragraph below the second list item.
- And here's the third list item.

Blockquotes

Markdown
```
* This is the first list item.
* Here's the second list item.

    > A blockquote would look great here.

* And here's the third list item.
```

HTML
```
<ul>
  <li><p>This is the first list item.</p></li>
  <li><p>Here's the second list item.</p>
    <blockquote>
      <p>A blockquote would look great here.</p>
    </blockquote>
  </li>
  <li><p>And here's the third list item.</p>
  </li>
</ul>
```

The rendered output looks like this:

- This is the first list item.
- Here's the second list item.

  > A blockquote would look great here.

- And here's the third list item.

Code Blocks

Code blocks are normally indented four spaces or one tab. When they're in a list, indent them eight spaces or two tabs.

Markdown

```
1. Open the file.
2. Find the following code block on line 21:

        <html>
          <head>
            <title>Test</title>
          </head>

3. Update the title to match the name of your website.
```

HTML

```
<ol>
  <li><p>Open the file.</p></li>
  <li><p>Find the following code block on line 21:</p>
    <pre><code>&lt;html&gt;
      &lt;head&gt;
        &lt;title&gt;Test&lt;/title&gt;
      &lt;/head&gt;
    </code></pre>
  </li>
  <li><p>Update the title to match the name of your websi\
te.</p></li>
</ol>
```

The rendered output looks like this:

1. Open the file.
2. Find the following code block on line 21:

```
<html>
  <head>
    <title>Test</title>
  </head>
```

3. Update the title to match the name of your website.

Images

Markdown

```
1. Open the file containing Tux, the Linux mascot.
2. Marvel at its beauty.

    ![Tux](images/tux.png)

3. Close the file.
```

HTML

```
<ol>
  <li><p>Open the file containing Tux, the Linux mascot.<\
/p></li>
  <li>
    <p>Marvel at its beauty.</p>
    <p><img src="images/tux.png" alt="Tux" /></p>
  </li>
  <li><p>Close the file.</p></li>
</ol>
```

The rendered output looks like this:

1. Open the file containing Tux, the Linux mascot.
2. Marvel at its beauty.

Tux

3. Close the file.

Lists

You can nest an unordered list in an ordered list, or vice versa.

Markdown

```
1. First item
2. Second item
3. Third item
    - Indented item
    - Indented item
4. Fourth item
```

HTML

```
<ol>
  <li>First item</li>
  <li>Second item</li>
  <li>Third item
    <ul>
      <li>Indented item</li>
      <li>Indented item</li>
    </ul>
  </li>
  <li>Fourth item</li>
</ol>
```

The rendered output looks like this:

1. First item
2. Second item
3. Third item
   - Indented item
   - Indented item
4. Fourth item

Code

To denote a word or phrase as code, enclose it in backticks (`` ` ``).

Markdown

```
At the command prompt, type `nano`.
```

HTML

```
At the command prompt, type <code>nano</code>.
```

The rendered output looks like this:

At the command prompt, type `nano`.

Escaping Backticks

If the word or phrase you want to denote as code includes one or more backticks, you can escape it by enclosing the word or phrase in double backticks.

Markdown

```
``Use `code` in your Markdown file.``
```

HTML

```
<code>Use `code` in your Markdown file.</code>
```

The rendered output looks like this:

```
Use `code` in your Markdown file.
```

Code Blocks

To create code blocks, indent every line of the block by at least four spaces or one tab.

Markdown

```
<html>
  <head>
  </head>
</html>
```

HTML

```
<pre>
  <code>
    &lt;html&gt;
      &lt;head&gt;
      &lt;/head&gt;
    &lt;/html&gt;
  </code>
</pre>
```

The rendered output looks like this:

```
<html>
  <head>
  </head>
</html>
```

 To create code blocks without indenting lines, use fenced code blocks. See Chapter 4 for more information.

Horizontal Rules

To create a horizontal rule, use three or more asterisks (***), dashes (---), or underscores (___) on a line by themselves.

Markdown

```
***


---


_____
```

HTML

```
<hr />


<hr />


<hr />
```

The rendered output of all three looks identical:

Horizontal Rule Best Practices

For compatibility, put blank lines before and after horizontal rules.

Do this:

Markdown
```
Try to put a blank line before...


---


...and after a horizontal rule.
```

Don't do this:

Markdown
```
Without blank lines, this would be a heading.
---
Don't do this!
```

Links

To create a link, enclose the link text in brackets (e.g., [Duck Duck Go]) and then follow it immediately with the URL in parentheses (e.g., (https://duckduckgo.com)).

Markdown
```
Use [Duck Duck Go](https://duckduckgo.com).
```

HTML
```
Use <a href="https://duckduckgo.com">Duck Duck Go</a>.
```

The rendered output looks like this:

Use Duck Duck Go[1].

---
[1]https://duckduckgo.com

Adding Titles

You can optionally add a title for a link. This will appear as a tooltip when the user hovers over the link. To add a title, enclose it in parentheses after the URL.

Markdown
```
Use [Duck Duck Go](https://duckduckgo.com "My search engi\
ne!").
```

HTML
```
Use <a href="https://duckduckgo.com" title="My search eng\
ine!">Duck Duck Go</a>.
```

The rendered output looks like this:

Use Duck Duck Go[2].

URLs and Email Addresses

To quickly turn a URL or email address into a link, enclose it in angle brackets.

Markdown
```
<https://eff.org>
<fake@example.com>
```

HTML
```
<a href="https://eff.org">https://eff.org</a>
<a href="mailto:fake@example.com">fake@example.com</a>
```

The rendered output looks like this:

https://eff.org
fake@example.com

---

[2]https://duckduckgo.com

Formatting Links

To emphasize links, add asterisks before and after the brackets and parentheses. To denote links as code, add backticks in the brackets.

Markdown

```
I love supporting **[EFF](https://eff.org)**.
This is the *[EFF](https://eff.org)*.
See the section on [`code`](#code).
```

HTML

```
I love supporting <strong><a href="https://eff.org">EFF</\
a></strong>.
This is the <em><a href="https://eff.org">EFF</a></em>.
See the section on <a href="#code"><code>code</code></a>.
```

The rendered output looks like this:

I love supporting **EFF**[3].
This is the *EFF*[4]. See the section on code.

Reference-style Links

Reference-style links are a special kind of link that make URLs easier to display and read in Markdown. Reference-style links are constructed in two parts: the part you keep inline with your text and the part you store somewhere else in the file to keep the text easy to read.

Formatting the First Part of the Link

The first part of a reference-style link is formatted with two sets of brackets. The first set of brackets surrounds the text that should

---

[3]https://eff.org
[4]https://eff.org

appear linked. The second set of brackets displays a label used to point to the link you're storing elsewhere in your document.

Although not required, you can include a space between the first and second set of brackets. Also, the label in the second set of brackets is not case sensitive and can include letters, numbers, spaces, or punctuation.

This means the following example formats are all roughly equivalent for the first part of the link:

Markdown

```
[hobbit-hole][1]
[hobbit-hole] [1]
[hobbit-hole][a]
[hobbit-hole][A]
```

Formatting the Second Part of the Link

The second part of a reference-style link is formatted with the following attributes:

1. The label, in brackets, followed immediately by a colon and at least one space (e.g., `[label]:`).
2. The URL for the link, which you can optionally enclose in angle brackets.
3. The optional title for the link, which you can enclose in double quotes, single quotes, or parentheses.

This means the following example formats are all roughly equivalent for the second part of the link:

Markdown

```
[hobbit-hole]: https://example.org/Hobbit#Lifestyle
[hobbit-hole]: https://example.org/Hobbit#Lifestyle "Hobb\
it lifestyles"
[hobbit-hole]: https://example.org/Hobbit#Lifestyle 'Hobb\
it lifestyles'
[hobbit-hole]: https://example.org/Hobbit#Lifestyle (Hobb\
it lifestyles)
[hobbit-hole]: <https://example.org/Hobbit#Lifestyle> "Ho\
bbit lifestyles"
[hobbit-hole]: <https://example.org/Hobbit#Lifestyle> 'Ho\
bbit lifestyles'
[hobbit-hole]: <https://example.org/Hobbit#Lifestyle> (Ho\
bbit lifestyles)
```

You can place this second part of the link anywhere in your
Markdown document. Some people place them immediately after
the paragraph in which they appear while other people place them
at the end of the document (like endnotes or footnotes).

An Example Putting the Parts Together

Say you add a URL as a standard URL link to a paragraph and it
looks like this in Markdown:

Markdown

```
In a hole in the ground there lived a hobbit. Not a nasty\
, dirty, wet hole, filled with the ends of worms and an o\
ozy smell, nor yet a dry, bare, sandy hole with nothing i\
n it to sit down on or to eat: it was a [hobbit-hole](htt\
ps://example.org/Hobbit#Lifestyle "Hobbit lifestyles"), a\
nd that means comfort.
```

Markdown

```
In a hole in the ground there lived a hobbit. Not a nasty\
, dirty, wet hole, filled with the ends of worms and an o\
ozy smell, nor yet a dry, bare, sandy hole with nothing i\
n it to sit down on or to eat: it was a [hobbit-hole][1],\
 and that means comfort.

[1]: <https://example.org/Hobbit#Lifestyle> "Hobbit lifes\
tyles"
```

In both instances above, the HTML for the link would be identical:

HTML

```
<a href="https://example.org/Hobbit#Lifestyle" title="Hob\
bit lifestyles">hobbit-hole</a>
```

The output is also identical:

In a hole in the ground there lived a hobbit. Not a nasty, dirty, wet
hole, filled with the ends of worms and an oozy smell, nor yet a dry,
bare, sandy hole with nothing in it to sit down on or to eat: it was
a hobbit-hole[5], and that means comfort.

Link Best Practices

Markdown applications don't agree on how to handle spaces in the
middle of a URL. For compatibility, try to URL encode any spaces
with %20.

Do this:

---

[5]https://example.org/Hobbit#Lifestyle

Markdown

```
[link](https://www.example.com/my%20great%20page)
```

Don't do this:

Markdown

```
[link](https://www.example.com/my great page)
```

Images

To add an image, add an exclamation mark (!), followed by alt text in brackets, and the path or URL to the image asset in parentheses. You can optionally add a title after the URL in the parentheses.

Markdown

```
![The San Juan Mountains are beautiful!](images/san-juan-\
mountains.jpg "San Juan Mountains")
```

HTML

```
<img src="images/san-juan-mountains.jpg" alt="The San Jua\
n Mountains are beautiful!" title="San Juan Mountains" />
```

The rendered output looks like this:

The San Juan Mountains are beautiful!

Linking Images

To add a link to an image, enclose the Markdown for the image in brackets, and then add the link in parentheses.

Markdown

```
[![An old rock in the desert](images/shiprock.jpg)](https\
://en.wikipedia.org/wiki/Shiprock)
```

HTML

```
<a href="https://en.wikipedia.org/wiki/Shiprock"><img src\
="images/shiprock.jpg" alt="An old rock in the desert"></\
a>
```

Escaping Characters

To display a literal character that would otherwise be used to format text in a Markdown document, add a backslash (\) in front of the character.

Markdown

```
\* Without the backslash, this would be a bullet in an un\
ordered list.
```

HTML

```
* Without the backslash, this would be a bullet in an uno\
rdered list.
```

The rendered output looks like this:

* Without the backslash, this would be a bullet in an unordered list.

Characters You Can Escape

You can use a backslash to escape the following characters.

Character	Name
\	backslash
`	backtick (see also escaping backticks in code)
*	asterisk
_	underscore
{}	curly braces
[]	brackets
<>	angle brackets
()	parentheses
#	pound sign
+	plus sign
-	minus sign (hyphen)
.	dot
!	exclamation mark
|	pipe (see also escaping pipe in tables)

HTML

Many Markdown applications allow you to use HTML tags in Markdown-formatted text. This is helpful if you prefer certain HTML tags to Markdown syntax. For example, some people find it easier to use HTML tags for images. Using HTML is also helpful when you need to change the attributes of an element, like specifying the color of text or changing the width of an image.

To use HTML, place the tags in the text of your Markdown-formatted file.

Markdown
```
This **word** is bold. This <em>word</em> is italic.
```

HTML
```
This <strong>word</strong> is bold. This <em>word</em> is\
 italic.
```

The rendered output looks like this:

This **word** is bold. This *word* is italic.

HTML Best Practices

For security reasons, not all Markdown applications support HTML in Markdown documents. When in doubt, check your Markdown application's documentation. Some applications support only a subset of HTML tags.

Use blank lines to separate block-level HTML elements like `<div>`, `<table>`, `<pre>`, and `<p>` from the surrounding content. Try not to indent the tags with tabs or spaces — that can interfere with the formatting.

You can't use Markdown syntax inside block-level HTML tags. For example, `<p>italic and **bold**</p>` won't work.

4. Extended Syntax

The basic syntax outlined in John Gruber's original design document added many of the elements needed on a day-to-day basis, but it wasn't enough for some people. That's where extended syntax comes in.

Several individuals and organizations took it upon themselves to extend the basic syntax by adding additional elements like tables, code blocks, syntax highlighting, URL auto-linking, and footnotes. These elements can be enabled by using a lightweight markup language that builds upon the basic Markdown syntax, or by adding an extension to a compatible Markdown processor.

Availability

Not all Markdown applications support extended syntax elements. You'll need to check whether or not the lightweight markup language your application is using supports the extended syntax elements you want to use. If it doesn't, it may still be possible to enable extensions in your Markdown processor.

Lightweight Markup Languages

There are several lightweight markup languages that are *supersets* of Markdown. They include Gruber's basic syntax and build upon it by adding additional elements like tables, code blocks, syntax highlighting, URL auto-linking, and footnotes. Many of the most popular Markdown applications use one of the following lightweight markup languages:

- CommonMark[1]
- GitHub Flavored Markdown[2]
- Markdown Extra[3]
- MultiMarkdown[4]
- R Markdown[5]

Markdown Processors

There are dozens of Markdown processors available. Many of them allow you to add extensions that enable extended syntax elements. Check your processor's documentation for more information.

Tables

To add a table, use three or more hyphens (---) to create each column's header, and use pipes (|) to separate each column. For compatibility, you should also add a pipe on either end of the row.

Markdown

```
| Syntax      | Description |
| ----------- | ----------- |
| Header      | Title       |
| Paragraph   | Text        |
```

[1]http://commonmark.org/
[2]https://github.github.com/gfm/
[3]https://michelf.ca/projects/php-markdown/extra/
[4]http://fletcherpenney.net/multimarkdown/
[5]https://rmarkdown.rstudio.com/

HTML

```
<table>
  <thead>
    <tr class="header">
      <th>Syntax</th>
      <th>Description</th>
    </tr>
  </thead>
  <tbody>
    <tr class="odd">
      <td>Header</td>
      <td>Title</td>
    </tr>
    <tr class="even">
      <td>Paragraph</td>
      <td>Text</td>
    </tr>
  </tbody>
</table>
```

The rendered output looks like this:

Syntax	Description
Header	Title
Paragraph	Text

Cell widths can vary, as shown below. The rendered output will look the same.

Markdown

```
| Syntax | Description |
| --- | ----------- |
| Header | Title |
| Paragraph | Text |
```

 Creating tables with hyphens and pipes can be tedious. To speed up the process, try using the Markdown Tables Generator[6]. Build a table using the graphical interface, and then copy the generated Markdown-formatted text into your file.

Alignment

You can align text in the columns to the left, right, or center by adding a colon (:) to the left, right, or on both side of the hyphens within the header row.

Markdown

```
| Syntax    | Description | Test Text    |
| :---      |    :----:   |        ---:  |
| Header    | Title       | Here's this  |
| Paragraph | Text        | And more     |
```

---

[6]http://www.tablesgenerator.com/markdown_tables

HTML

```
<table>
  <thead>
    <tr class="header">
      <th style="text-align: left;">Syntax</th>
      <th style="text-align: center;">Description</th>
      <th style="text-align: right;">Test Text</th>
    </tr>
  </thead>
  <tbody>
    <tr class="odd">
      <td style="text-align: left;">Header</td>
      <td style="text-align: center;">Title</td>
      <td style="text-align: right;">Here's this</td>
    </tr>
    <tr class="even">
      <td style="text-align: left;">Paragraph</td>
      <td style="text-align: center;">Text</td>
      <td style="text-align: right;">And more</td>
    </tr>
  </tbody>
</table>
```

The rendered output looks like this:

Syntax	Description	Test Text
Header	Title	Here's this
Paragraph	Text	And more

Formatting Text in Tables

You can format the text within tables. For example, you can add links, code (words or phrases in backticks (`) only, not code blocks), and emphasis.

You can't add headings, blockquotes, lists, horizontal rules, images, or HTML tags.

Escaping Pipe Characters in Tables

You can display a pipe (|) character in a table by using its HTML character code (|).

Fenced Code Blocks

The basic Markdown syntax allows you to create code blocks by indenting lines by four spaces or one tab. If you find that inconvenient, try using fenced code blocks. Depending on your Markdown processor or editor, you'll use three backticks (```) or three tildes (~~~) on the lines before and after the code block. The best part? You don't have to indent any lines!

Markdown

```
{
  "firstName": "John",
  "lastName": "Smith",
  "age": 25
}
```

HTML

```
<pre>
  <code>
    {
      &quot;firstName&quot;: &quot;John&quot;,
      &quot;lastName&quot;: &quot;Smith&quot;,
      &quot;age&quot;: 25
    }
  </code>
</pre>
```

The rendered output looks like this:

```
{
  "firstName": "John",
  "lastName": "Smith",
  "age": 25
}
```

 Need to display backticks inside a code block? See the Escaping Characters section in Chapter 3 to learn how to escape them.

Syntax Highlighting

Many Markdown processors support syntax highlighting for fenced code blocks. This feature allows you to add color highlighting for whatever language your code was written in. To add syntax highlighting, specify a language next to the backticks before the fenced code block.

Markdown

```json
{
  "firstName": "John",
  "lastName": "Smith",
  "age": 25
}
```

HTML

```
<pre>
  <code class="language-json">
    {
      &quot;firstName&quot;: &quot;John&quot;,
      &quot;lastName&quot;: &quot;Smith&quot;,
      &quot;age&quot;: 25
    }
  </code>
</pre>
```

Footnotes

Footnotes allow you to add notes and references without cluttering the body of the document. When you create a footnote, a superscript number with a link appears where you added the footnote reference. Readers can click the link to jump to the content of the footnote at the bottom of the page.

To create a footnote reference, add a caret and an identifier inside brackets ([^1]). Identifiers can be numbers or words, but they can't contain spaces or tabs. Identifiers only correlate the footnote reference with the footnote itself — in the output, footnotes are numbered sequentially.

Add the footnote using another caret and number inside brackets with a colon and text ([^1]: My footnote.). You don't have to put footnotes at the end of the document. You can put them anywhere except inside other elements like lists, block quotes, and tables.

Markdown

```
Here's a simple footnote,[^1] and here's a longer one.[^b\
ignote]

[^1]: This is the first footnote.

[^bignote]: Here's one with multiple paragraphs and code.

    Indent paragraphs to include them in the footnote.

    `{ my code }`

    Add as many paragraphs as you like.
```

HTML

```
<p>
  Here's a simple footnote,<a href="#fn1" class="footnote\
-ref" id="fnref1"><sup>1</sup></a> and here's a longer on\
e.<a href="#fn2" class="footnote-ref" id="fnref2"><sup>2<\
/sup></a>
</p>
<section class="footnotes">
  <hr />
  <ol>
    <li id="fn1"><p>This is the first footnote.<a href="#\
fnref1" class="footnote-back">&#8617;&#xFE0E;</a></p></li\
>
    <li id="fn2">
      <p>Here's one with multiple paragraphs and code.</p>
      <p>Indent paragraphs to include them in the footnot\
```

```
e.</p>
     <p><code>{ my code }</code></p>
     <p>Add as many paragraphs as you like.<a href="#fnr\
ef2" class="footnote-back">&#8617;&#xFE0E;</a></p>
   </li>
 </ol>
</section>
```

The rendered output looks like this:

Here's a simple footnote,[7] and here's a longer one.[8]

Heading IDs

Many Markdown processors support custom IDs for headings
— some Markdown processors automatically add them. Adding
custom IDs allows you to link directly to headings and modify them
with CSS. To add a custom heading ID, enclose the custom ID in
curly braces on the same line as the heading.

Markdown

```
### My Great Heading {#custom-id}
```

HTML

```
<h3 id="custom-id">My Great Heading</h3>
```

---

[7]This is the first footnote.
[8]Here's one with multiple paragraphs and code.
Indent paragraphs to include them in the footnote.
{ my code }
Add as many paragraphs as you like.

Linking to Heading IDs

You can link to headings with custom IDs in the file by creating a standard link with a number sign (#) followed by the custom heading ID.

Markdown

```
[Heading IDs](#heading-ids)
```

HTML

```
<a href="#heading-ids">Heading IDs</a>
```

Other websites can link to the heading by adding the custom heading ID to the full URL of the webpage (e.g, `[Heading IDs](https://www.eff.org/page#heading-ids)`).

Definition Lists

Some Markdown processors allow you to create *definition lists* of terms and their corresponding definitions. To create a definition list, type the term on the first line. On the next line, type a colon followed by a space and the definition.

Markdown

```
First Term
: This is the definition of the first term.

Second Term
: This is one definition of the second term.
: This is another definition of the second term.
```

HTML

```
<dl>
  <dt>First Term</dt>
  <dd>This is the definition of the first term.</dd>
  <dt>Second Term</dt>
  <dd>This is one definition of the second term. </dd>
  <dd>This is another definition of the second term.</dd>
</dl>
```

The rendered output looks like this:

First Term
    This is the definition of the first term.
Second Term
    This is one definition of the second term.

    This is another definition of the second term.

Strikethrough

You can "strikethrough" words by putting a horizontal line through the center of them. This feature allows you to indicate that certain words are a mistake not meant for inclusion in the document. To strikethrough words, use two tilde symbols (~~) before and after the words.

Markdown

```
The world is ~~flat~~ round.
```

HTML

```
<p>The world is <del>flat</del> round.</p>
```

The rendered output looks like this:

The world is ~~flat~~ round.

Task Lists

Task lists allow you to create a list of items with checkboxes. In Markdown applications that support task lists, checkboxes will be displayed next to the content. To create a task list, add dashes (-) and brackets with a space ([ ]) in front of task list items. To select a checkbox, add an x in between the brackets ([x]).

Markdown

```
- [x] Write the press release
- [ ] Update the website
- [ ] Contact the media
```

The rendered output looks like this:

     ✓ Write the press release
       Update the website
       Contact the media

Task list

Emoji

There are two ways to add emoji to Markdown files: copy and paste the emoji into your Markdown-formatted text, or type *emoji shortcodes*.

Copying and Pasting Emoji

In most cases, you can simply copy an emoji from a source like Emojipedia[9] and paste it into your document. Many Markdown applications will automatically display the emoji in the Markdown-formatted text. The HTML and PDF files you export from your Markdown application should display the emoji.

 If you're using a static site generator, make sure you encode HTML pages as UTF-8[10].

Using Emoji Shortcodes

Some Markdown applications allow you to insert emoji by typing emoji shortcodes. These begin and end with a colon and include the name of an emoji.

Markdown
```
Gone camping! :tent: Be back soon.

That is so funny! :joy:
```

 There are lists of emoji shortcodes[11] available, but keep in mind that emoji shortcodes vary from application to application. Refer to your Markdown application's documentation for more information.

---

[9]https://emojipedia.org/
[10]https://www.w3.org/International/tutorials/tutorial-char-enc/
[11]https://gist.github.com/rxaviers/7360908

Automatic URL Linking

Many Markdown processors automatically turn URLs into links. That means if you type http://www.example.com, your Markdown processor will automatically turn it into a link even though you haven't used brackets.

Markdown

```
http://example.com
```

HTML

```
<a href="http://example.com">http://example.com</a>
```

The rendered output looks like this:

http://example.com

Disabling Automatic URL Linking

If you don't want a URL to be automatically linked, you can remove the link by denoting the URL as code with backticks.

Markdown

```
`http://www.example.com`
```

HTML

```
<code>http://www.example.com</code>
```

The rendered output looks like this:

```
http://www.example.com
```

5. Cheat Sheet

This cheat sheet provides a quick overview of all the Markdown syntax elements. It can't cover every edge case! If you need more information about any of these elements, refer back to the chapters on basic and extended syntax.

Basic Syntax

These are the elements outlined in John Gruber's original design document. All Markdown applications support these elements.

Element	Markdown Syntax
Heading	`# H1`
	`## H2`
	`### H3`
Bold	`**bold text**`
Italic	`*italicized text*`
Blockquote	`> blockquote`
Ordered List	`1. First item`
	`2. Second item`
	`3. Third item`
Unordered List	`- First item`
	`- Second item`
	`- Third item`
Code	`` `code` ``
Horizontal Rule	`---`
Link	`[title](https://www.example.com)`
Image	`![alt text](image.jpg)`

Extended Syntax

These elements extend the basic syntax by adding additional features. Not all Markdown applications support these elements.

Element	Markdown Syntax

Table	`| Syntax | Description |`
	`| ------ | ----------- |`
	`| Header | Title |`
	`| Paragraph | Text |`

Fenced Code Block	` ``` ` `{` `"firstName": "John",` `"lastName": "Smith",` `"age": 25` `}` ` ``` `

Footnote	`Here's a sentence with a`
	`footnote. [^1]`
	
	`[^1]: This is the footnote.`

Heading ID	`### My Great Heading` `{#custom-id}`
Definition List	`term` `: definition`
Strikethrough	`~~The world is flat.~~`

Task List	`- [x] Write the press release`
	`- [ ] Update the website`
	`- [ ] Contact the media`

About the Author

Matt Cone is a technical writer at Fastly. He has experience creating documentation for organizations like Linode and the U.S. Department of Health and Human Services. Matt's first book, *Master Your Mac*, was published by No Starch Press. To get in touch with Matt, visit https://www.mattcone.com.

www.ingramcontent.com/pod-product-compliance
Lightning Source LLC
LaVergne TN
LVHW041219050326
832903LV00021B/693